Try Something New

for Families

100 Fun & Creative Ways to Spend Time Together

Published by Neuron Publishing
www.neuronpublishing.com
www.LoveBookOnline.com

 LoveBook®

#1 - Extend a helping hand for the holidays

Volunteer with organizations in your area to deliver Thanksgiving baskets, adopt a family for Christmas, or invite an out-of-towner to join your family for a holiday meal.

Which holiday did you pick? _____
_____

Who did you decide to help? Why? _____
_____

How did you help them? _____
_____

How would you rank this? ☆☆☆☆☆ Why? _____
_____

1

#2 - Create a yearly family scrapbook

Have each person create pages for another family member. Include photos, quotes and memorabilia for their interests, accomplishments, and activities from the previous year.

What did you learn about your family? _____

_____

What was your favorite memory from the year? _____

_____

How did the final scrapbook turn out? _____

_____

How would you rank this? ☆ ☆ ☆ ☆ ☆ Why? _____

_____

Completed:

_____

#3 - Name that sound

Pick one person to record everyday and unusual sounds from your home, neighborhood, and city. Play them back and see who can guess the most sounds correctly. Bonus points for guessing the location.

Who guessed the most sounds? _____

_____

Which was the hardest to guess? _____

_____

Did you start listening more carefully to your surroundings?

_____

How would you rank this? ☆☆☆☆☆ Why? _____

_____

Completed:
_____

#4 - See the best in the ones you love

One day a month make an effort to say at least three nice and meaningful things to each member of your family. Pick different days and spread the love throughout the entire month.

Which compliment had the biggest impact? _____
_____

How did it affect the mood in your house? _____
_____

Is this something you would want to do more often? _____

How would you rank this? ★ ★ ★ ★ ★ Why? _____
_____

#5 - Plot your course

Create a backyard treasure hunt. Visit the dollar store for 'treasures', create a map, and make clues for how to find them. If you're feeling ambitious extend the hunt to the neighborhood and invite the neighbors.

What treasures did you bury? _____

_____

Who found them? Where? _____

_____

What was the hardest clue to figure out? _____

_____

How would you rank this? ☆ ☆ ☆ ☆ ☆ Why? _____

_____

Completed:
_____

#6 - Create a work of art one line at a time

Decide on a topic. Then grab some crayons or colored pencils and a large piece of paper. Take turns drawing a line and then pass the paper until the drawing is completed.

What category did you choose? _____
_____

How did the final drawing compare to the original idea? _____
_____

Is anyone naturally talented at drawing? _____
_____

How would you rank this? ☆☆☆☆☆ Why? _____
_____

6

#7 - Host your very own Olympic Games

Set up in a nearby park or your own backyard. Pick age/skill level appropriate races and events so everyone can be involved. Give prizes to the winners and encourage good sportsmanship.

①

Which games/events did you have? _____
_____

What was everyone's best event? _____
_____

Were there any surprises or upsets? _____
_____

How would you rank this? ☆☆☆☆☆ Why? _____
_____

7

#8 - Follow the leader

Go for a walk as a family around your neighborhood. At the corners and intersections have each person take a turn deciding which way to go. You never know what fun destination lies right around the corner.

Did you discover anything new in your neighborhood? _____
_____

What was your favorite part of the walk? _____
_____

Who had the most fun being the leader? _____
_____

How would you rank this? ☆ ☆ ☆ ☆ ☆ Why? _____
_____

#9 - Take a walk in someone else's shoes

Shadow another member of your family for a day. With appropriate permission, join them in their daily routine whether at school, work, on errands, or wherever the day takes you.

Who did you shadow and what did you do? _____
_____

What did you learn about that person? _____
_____

How did it change your perspective? _____
_____

How would you rank this? ☆ ☆ ☆ ☆ ☆ Why? _____
_____

#10 - Cheer on a new team in person

Find a sporting event or team that you've never seen play live. It can be a professional team, college, minor, or even a rec league. Go to the game, root on the team, and have fun!

Which sport and team did you pick? _____

_____

Did the team win? Was it an exciting game? _____

_____

Would you watch this team play again? _____

_____

How would you rank this? ★ ★ ★ ★ ★ Why? _____

_____

#11 - Construct your own little world

Work together to build a fort in your house. Use blocks, blankets, furniture, or whatever you have. Spend the day playing inside it, watching movies, eating meals, and then camp for the night.

What did you make your fort out of? _____
_____

What did you do inside? _____
_____

What was your favorite part of the day? _____
_____

How would you rank this? ☆ ☆ ☆ ☆ ☆ Why? _____
_____

Completed:
_____

#12 - Create a club just for readers

Get your family excited to read by forming a book club. Take turns picking a book that you can all read together and talk about. Younger kids can read along with their parents.

Which book did you chose first? _____
_____

What did you discuss about the book? _____
_____

Did everyone like reading it? _____
_____

How would you rank this? ☆ ☆ ☆ ☆ ☆ Why? _____
_____

12

#13 - Take flight

Get a kite, rocket, or airplane kit and build it together. Customize it with paint and decals that represent your family. On the next windy day host a launch party in your backyard or at a nearby park.

What did you build? _____
_____

How well did it fly? _____
_____

What would you do differently if you built another one? _____
_____

How would you rank this? ☆☆☆☆☆ Why? _____
_____

#14 - Dance like you just don't care

Push your furniture aside and make room for a dance party. Make playlists of your favorite songs and take turns being DJ. Get everyone out on the floor to show off their best moves.

Was everyone able to let loose and have a good time? _____
_____

Who had the best dance move? _____
_____

What was the favorite song of the night? _____
_____

How would you rank this? ☆ ☆ ☆ ☆ ☆ Why? _____
_____

#15 - Shout 'Action'!

Shoot your own movie. Collaborate on a short script and assign actors for the parts. Pick someone to direct and a person to shoot it on your home camcorder or phone. Then invite friends over for a screening party.

What genre of movie did you make? What did you title it?
_____

Who directed, who acted, and who shot the movie? _____
_____

How did the final movie turn out? _____
_____

How would you rank this? ☆☆☆☆☆ Why? _____
_____

#16 - Author a family favorites cookbook

Have each person pick five of their favorite recipes, write them up, and put them in a binder. As you make the recipes, take pictures and add them to the cookbook.

Which recipe was the overall, family favorite? _____
_____

Who, in the family, enjoys cooking? _____
_____

Have you added more recipes since you made the cookbook?
_____

How would you rank this? ★ ★ ★ ★ ★ Why? _____
_____

#17 - Break out the paper mache

Host a festive fiesta night for your family and friends. Make a paper mache pinata, put together a taco bar, and play some festive music. Invite your guests to come in costume.

How did everyone get involved with the party planning? _____
_____

Was it a fun theme for your family and guests? _____
_____

Who had the best costume? _____
_____

How would you rank this? ☆☆☆☆☆ Why? _____
_____

#18 - Grow your food

Plant a vegetable garden. Choose some vegetables your kids already like and add in a few new varieties. Get everyone involved with planting, weeding, watering, and harvesting so they can take pride in the end result.

What did you decide to grow? _____
_____

How did each person participate? _____
_____

How did they react to eating the vegetables they grew? _____
_____

How would you rank this? ☆☆☆☆☆ Why? _____
_____

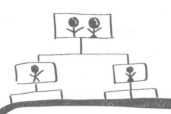

#19 - Draw out your family's history

Make a family tree out of construction paper, scissors, glue, and markers. List as many family members as you can and include pictures. Get grandparents to help if possible.

How far back were you able to go? _____
_____

What did you learn about your family's history? _____
_____

What did you teach your kids about your family? _____
_____

How would you rank this? ☆☆☆☆☆ Why? _____
_____

#20 - Wake up your family's taste buds

Once a week, have someone choose a new recipe (use the internet, cooking shows, etc), help shop for the ingredients, and make the meal. If it's a hit, add it to your favorites cookbook.

Did this inspire any new chefs in your family? _____
_____

What has your family learned from cooking? _____
_____

What is your family's most requested meal? _____
_____

How would you rank this? ☆ ☆ ☆ ☆ ☆ Why? _____
_____

#21 - Capture your year in pictures

Head to a local park or just your own backyard. Take a picture of your family. Take the same picture again every month for a year and see how the seasons and your family changes.

Where did you take the picture? _____
_____

What was the biggest change you noticed? _____
_____

Will you try to continue this the following year? _____
_____

How would you rank this? ☆☆☆☆☆ Why? _____
_____

Completed:
_____

#22 - Expand your horizons from home

Pick a faraway destination. Research the culture, food, weather, etc. Make a collage board with images representing the region. Find a restaurant that serves the region's foods or make your own.

Which destination did you pick? Why? _____

_____

What was the most interesting thing you learned? _____

_____

Would you consider visiting this place? Why? _____

_____

How would you rank this? ★ ★ ★ ★ ★ Why? _____

_____

#23 - Meet your neighborhood heroes

Arrange a tour for your kids at your local fire station. Take them to meet the firefighters, see the truck and all the gear, and learn important fire safety tips.

What did your kids think of the firehouse? _____
_____

What was the most important thing they learned? _____
_____

What is your family's plan in the event of a fire? _____
_____

How would you rank this? ☆☆☆☆☆ Why? _____
_____

Completed:

_____

#24 - Eat off a stick

Plan a fun, family meal that includes only things that are served on a stick. Make fondue, grill kabobs, roast marshmallows, and look for corn dogs in the freezer section of the grocery store. Have a little fun with your food!

What did you serve? _____

_____

How did this compare to your usual family dinners? _____

_____

What other themed dinners might you have? _____

_____

How would you rank this? ☆☆☆☆☆ Why? _____

_____

#25 - Send them your thanks and support

Show your gratitude by writing letters, drawing pictures, and sending cards to soldiers serving overseas. Look online to find charitable organizations and directions for sending your mail.

What types of mail did you send? _____
_____

What kind of impact has this had on your family? _____
_____

Have you received any responses? _____
_____

How would you rank this? ☆☆☆☆☆ Why? _____
_____

#26 - Show someone special that you care

Work together to bake your favorite homemade treats. Wrap them up along with a handmade card and deliver them to an elderly neighbor or relative who doesn't get many visitors.

What did you decide to make? _____
_____

Who did you choose to deliver them to? Why? _____
_____

How did the person react? _____
_____

How would you rank this? ☆ ☆ ☆ ☆ ☆ Why? _____
_____

#27 - Put your science skills to the test

Host your own science fair. Research projects that the family can work on together. Invite some families over to participate and get someone to judge. Hand out blue ribbons to the winners.

1

What projects were presented? _____
_____

Which project took first place? Why? _____
_____

What did your family learn from the project? _____
_____

How would you rank this? ☆☆☆☆☆ Why? _____
_____

Completed:
_____

#28 - Send each other some snail mail

Make a family mailbox. Grab a cardboard box, cut a slit in the top, and decorate it. Leave each other notes, cards, letters, pictures, etc. Take turns checking the mailbox and handing out the mail.

How did you decorate your mailbox? _____
_____

What kinds of things have you sent each other? _____
_____

What does your family think of this non-electronic mail? _____
_____

How would you rank this? ★ ★ ★ ★ ★ Why? _____
_____

#29 - Plan a surprise picnic lunch

Pack some of their favorite foods and surprise your child at school or day care. Take them out to a nearby park or your favorite spot for a picnic and a little extra one-on-one time together.

Was your child surprised? _____

_____

Where did you go together? _____

_____

Who else in your family would enjoy this? _____

_____

How would you rank this? ☆ ☆ ☆ ☆ ☆ Why? _____

_____

#30 - Spice up your family movie night

Choose the move and write up a handful of questions about it ahead of time. Stop it every 30 min. or so and see who can buzz in and answer the fastest. Have prizes for the winners.

Which movie did you watch? _____

_____

What was the hardest question asked? _____

_____

Who answered the most questions correctly? _____

_____

How would you rank this? ☆☆☆☆☆ Why? _____

_____

#31 - Publish a family newsletter

Give everyone a job: writing articles, taking pictures, laying out the pages on the computer, etc. Send it out to your extended family and friends to let them know what you are up to.

How did everyone contribute? _____

_____

What was each person's favorite part? _____

_____

What kind of feedback did you get after sending it? _____

_____

How would you rank this? ☆☆☆☆☆ Why? _____

_____

Completed:
_____

#32 - Step outside your comfort zone

Do something that scares you. Make a list of activities that are safe but challenging for each person. Then make a plan to help each other achieve it and celebrate their success.

What does the list look like? _____

_____

Did everyone achieve their goal? _____

_____

Did it help anyone overcome their fear? _____

_____

How would you rank this? ☆ ☆ ☆ ☆ ☆ Why? _____

_____

#33 - Turn your dreams into a reality

As a family, pick a big goal (vacation, big purchase, etc.), and make a savings jar. Decorate the jar with images of what you're saving for, place it in a central location, and work together to earn it.

What did you decide to put your savings toward? _____
_____

How did you decorate the jar? _____
_____

Did you reach your goal? How long did it take? _____
_____

How would you rank this? ☆ ☆ ☆ ☆ ☆ Why? _____
_____

#34 - Start a 'best of' list for your city

Make your own survey sheets for the different places you visit. The next time you're out to eat, at a movie, or in a park decide which has the best pizza, buttered popcorn, or tire swing. ★★★★☆

What criteria did you put on the surveys? _____

_____

Did everyone agree on the winners? _____

_____

How does the list impact where you go? _____

_____

How would you rank this? ★ ★ ★ ★ ★ Why? _____

_____

#35 - Journey with no real destination

Hop on the nearest mode of public transportation. Take a ride on a bus, train, cable car, ferry, etc. Enjoy the sights and sounds, people watch, and then head back home.

What things did you see, smell, and hear? _____
_____

Were you able to just enjoy the ride? _____
_____

What are some other modes of transportation you could try?
_____

How would you rank this? ★ ★ ★ ★ ★ Why? _____
_____

#36 - Move those hips

Challenge the family to a hula-hoop competition. Use it as a chance to be silly and have a good time together. Once you've mastered it around your waist, try your arms, legs, and neck. Don't forget to crown the winner.

Who kept it going the longest? _____
_____

Was anyone able to get past their waist? _____
_____

What was the prize for the winner? _____
_____

How would you rank this? ☆ ☆ ☆ ☆ ☆ Why? _____
_____

#37 - Host an extreme room makeover

Make a deal with your kids. If they clean out their rooms, donate unused toys and clothes, then they get to pick out a new paint color and room decor. Work on transforming their rooms together.

Where did you decide to donate the toys and clothes? _____
_____

What color(s) did they choose? _____
_____

How did they decorate their new rooms? _____
_____

How would you rank this? ☆☆☆☆☆ Why? _____
_____

#38 - Put the kids in charge for a day

Plan a day when the kids get to make the decisions for all of the family's activities. Set a dollar and distance limit ahead of time to establish parameters, but everything else is up to them.

I'M IN CHARGE

What was the first thing the kids wanted to do? _____
_____

Were you surprised by anything they picked? _____
_____

Did everyone have a good time? _____
_____

How would you rank this? ☆ ☆ ☆ ☆ ☆ Why? _____
_____

#39 - Make a home for your flying friends

Build a birdhouse together. Get a kit or find plans online. Research what types of birds are in your area and what to feed them. Place the birdhouse outside where everyone can enjoy watching it.

What did you learn about birds in your area? _____

_____

Have you seen many birds near the birdhouse? Which kinds?

_____

What is your favorite that you've seen so far? _____

_____

How would you rank this? ☆☆☆☆☆ Why? _____

_____

Completed:
_____

#40 - Take a tour of your state capital

Do a little research online to find out about planning your trip and when tours are available. See your local government in action and learn some history and fun facts about your state.

★

What was the most interesting thing you learned? _____
_____

Did you see any public figures? Who? _____
_____

Is your family interested in visiting other capitals? Which ones?
_____

How would you rank this? ★ ★ ★ ★ ★ Why? _____
_____

40

OUR FAMILY

#41 - Brand yourselves

Make a list of things that describe your family's activities, beliefs and values. Pick your top two or three and come up with symbols to visually represent them. Then use the symbols together to draw your very own family crest.

What were your top three words to describe your family?

_____

How did you decide to represent them? _____

_____

What are some ways you could use your new family crest?

_____

How would you rank this? ☆ ☆ ☆ ☆ ☆ Why? _____

_____

Completed:
_____

#42 - Cool off with a family car wash

On the next hot day skip the pool, turn on some music, and make the family car shine. Have two cars? Split up into teams and make it a competition to see who can clean their car the fastest.

Did the car actually get cleaned or was it all fun? _____
_____

Did a competition get started? Who won? _____
_____

Would you consider this a good summer job for the kids?
_____

How would you rank this? ☆ ☆ ☆ ☆ ☆ Why? _____
_____

#43 - Design your dream house

Find images of rooms that you love from home design magazines or print online images. Pick your favorites and build your dream home by laying them out on the living room floor.

How did everyone's style differ? _____
_____

Did you get any design ideas for your current house? _____
_____

Which room is most important to each person? _____
_____

How would you rank this? ☆☆☆☆☆ Why? _____
_____

Completed:
_____

#44 - Buy local

Support local business and get fresh produce by exploring the farmer's market in your area. Have each family member pick out a food they've never tried before and then go home and make dinner with what you bought.

What did everyone pick? _____

_____

What did you make for dinner? _____

_____

Did you find a new family favorite? _____

_____

How would you rank this? ☆ ☆ ☆ ☆ ☆ Why? _____

_____

WELCOME

#45 - Open your doors

Show your family what it means to be welcoming. Make a big pot of chili and invite your neighbors/friends to drop by with their families for an impromptu potluck. Include those new to the area or to your group and widen your circle.

Who did you invite? _____
_____

What did you do together? _____
_____

Who could you invite in the future? _____
_____

How would you rank this? ☆ ☆ ☆ ☆ ☆ Why? _____
_____

#46 - Get them talking

Come up with some fun, thought provoking questions and put them on folded pieces of paper in a box. The next time dinner conversation is lagging, take turns picking a question and go around the table getting everyone's answer.

How did you come up with the questions? _____

_____

Did they spark any interesting conversations? _____

_____

What was the most thought provoking question? _____

_____

How would you rank this? ★ ★ ★ ★ ★ Why? _____

_____

#47 - Tour your town

Don't overlook your own city as a destination. Check out your area's tourism website for ideas. Make a list with your family of the things you're interested in and make a plan to start checking them off the list.

What are the top three places/activities on the list? _____
_____

Which was the favorite? _____
_____

What other things could you do in your area? _____
_____

How would you rank this? ☆ ☆ ☆ ☆ ☆ Why? _____
_____

Completed:
_____

#48 - Get creative with your footwear

Buy some canvas sneakers or use some you already own. Be crafty with gel pens, markers, glitter, fun laces, and start decorating! You'll have a cool reminder of your time spent together.

How did the shoes turn out? _____
_____

What was the inspiration for the designs? _____
_____

Will they be worn or displayed as artwork? _____
_____

How would you rank this? ☆ ☆ ☆ ☆ ☆ Why? _____
_____

#49 - Make up the rules as you go

For your next family game night, create your own games. Encourage everyone to come up with their own take on an existing game, or try their hand at creating an entirely new game.

How many new/reworked games did you come up with? _____
_____

Were they board games, card games, or sports based? _____
_____

Which would everyone play again? _____
_____

How would you rank this? ☆☆☆☆☆ Why? _____
_____

#50 - Tag somebody

Play laser tag! Look online to find a laser tag center in your area. Many have both indoor and outdoor fields. Grab your family and maybe some friends for a day full of friendly competition and exercise.

Did you play on a team together or against each other? _____
_____

Did everyone have a good time? _____
_____

Who was the most competitive? _____
_____

How would you rank this? ☆ ☆ ☆ ☆ ☆ Why? _____
_____

#51 - See a sky full of floating colors

Search online for a local hot air balloon launch. Pack up the family and head out for a day of fun! Some cities make a festival of it complete with food, games, and contests.

What was everyone's favorite balloon? _____
_____

What other activities did the family try? _____
_____

Did anyone get to ride in a balloon? _____
_____

How would you rank this? ☆ ☆ ☆ ☆ ☆ Why? _____
_____

Completed:

_____

#52 - Determine your own fortunes

Have everyone write out 2 or 3 fortunes on strips of paper. Look up the recipe for fortune cookies online and make them together. Serve them for dessert and read your fortunes aloud.

How did the cookies come out? _____

_____

What was the funniest fortune? _____

_____

Were any of the fortunes accurate? _____

_____

How would you rank this? ★ ★ ★ ★ ★ Why? _____

_____

#53 - Discover your true calling

Once a month a family member picks a profession he/she is interested in. Do some research on what the profession involves. Then try to set up a brief job shadowing of someone who has that job.

What are the professions that interest each of you? _____
_____

What was learned researching them? _____
_____

Did anyone change their mind after job shadowing? _____
_____

How would you rank this? ☆ ☆ ☆ ☆ ☆ Why? _____
_____

Completed:
_____

#54 - Draw your town

Look up a map of your area. On a large piece of paper draw a basic outline of the area and then have everyone fill in some favorite places: home, friend's/family's houses, schools, church, restaurants, parks etc.

What was learned about your town? _____

_____

Which places are on the map? _____

_____

What areas are left to be explored in your town? _____

_____

How would you rank this? ☆☆☆☆☆ Why? _____

_____

#55 - Hunt for bugs

Grab a shovel and bucket and head to the backyard or park. Look for worms, ladybugs, roly polys or whatever harmless bugs you can find. Place them in a ventilated box and research what they are, their habitat, etc.

What bugs were discovered? _____
_____

Where were they found? _____
_____

What was learned about them? _____
_____

How would you rank this? ☆☆☆☆☆ Why? _____
_____

#56 - Find your pair

Come up with a set of words that go together (i.e. peanut butter and jelly). Put each half on a piece of paper. Tape one on everyone's back. Ask questions to find out what is on your back, then try to find the person who is your pair.

Did everyone figure out what their word was? _____

_____

What was the hardest to figure out? _____

_____

Did everyone find their pair? _____

_____

How would you rank this? ★ ★ ★ ★ ★ Why? _____

_____

#57 - Show off your individual talents

Host a family talent show. Have everyone pick a talent they want to show off. Invite a friend to judge or video tape it and vote yourselves. Decide on different categories of winners and have prizes.

What were the family's talents? _____

_____

Who judged and what were the categories of winners? _____

_____

Who won? What were the prizes? _____

_____

How would you rank this? ☆ ☆ ☆ ☆ ☆ Why? _____

_____

Completed:

_____

#58 - Find what you're passionate about

Have each person pick a cause that is important to them (i.e. feed the hungry), then find activities to support that cause (i.e. volunteer at a food pantry). Make it a family event and get everyone involved.

What cause did each person pick? _____

_____

What is being done to support that cause? _____

_____

How has this impacted your family? _____

_____

How would you rank this? ★ ★ ★ ★ ★ Why? _____

_____

#59 - Celebrate the obscure things

Once a month one family member gets to pick a little known holiday. Search online for ideas (i.e. talk like a pirate day). Then have the whole family help to celebrate the day. Get as festive as you can!

What are some of the holidays that have been picked? _____

_____

What did you do to celebrate them? _____

_____

Have you decided to celebrate any of them annually? _____

_____

How would you rank this? ☆ ☆ ☆ ☆ ☆ Why? _____

_____

Completed:
_____

#60 - Throw a family pajama party

Pick a day when no one has to go anywhere and spend the whole day in your pajamas together. Play board games, watch movies, and eat your favorite snack foods.

How did it feel to have a day together with nothing you had to do?
_____

What did the family do together? _____
_____

Was it relaxing or were you all ready to get out of the house?
_____

How would you rank this? ☆☆☆☆☆ Why? _____
_____

#61 - Start a food fight

On the next nice day take your dinner outside. Sometime throughout the meal instigate a food fight. Go ahead and get messy. When you're done break out the garden hose to get everyone cleaned up before heading back inside.

How did the family react when the food fight started? _____
_____

Did everyone get involved? _____
_____

Who had the most fun getting messy? _____
_____

How would you rank this? ☆☆☆☆☆ Why? _____
_____

#62 - Work on your communication skills

For one day, communicate in a language other than your first language. It can be sign language, Pig Latin, or a completely made up language. See how well you really understand each other.

Which 'language' did you choose? _____

_____

What was the most challenging part? _____

_____

How did it affect your communication skills afterward? _____

_____

How would you rank this? ★ ★ ★ ★ ★ Why? _____

_____

#63 - Get fit together

Start your own boot camp at home. Set up stations for push up, crunches, suicides, squats etc. Challenge your family to do as many reps as they can. Keep track of time and reps and compare month to month.

What stations did you have? _____
_____

How did everyone do the first time through? _____
_____

Who was most improved? _____
_____

How would you rank this? ☆ ☆ ☆ ☆ ☆ Why? _____
_____

Completed:
_____

#64 - Be prepared

Make a family emergency plan. Talk about what you'll do and where you'll go. Put together a list of emergency contacts. Gather supplies (i.e. food, water, first aid, etc) and put together a family emergency kit.

MEET HERE

What emergencies did you plan for? _____

_____

Did you practice your plan and emergency routes? _____

_____

What else can you do to make sure everyone is prepared? _____

_____

How would you rank this? ★ ★ ★ ★ ★ Why? _____

_____

#65 - Make a list of your family goals

Work together to brainstorm a list of things that you would like to accomplish as a family. Write them down in a journal. Include time frames and what you'll need to reach each goal. Then get started!

What are the first three goals on the list? _____
_____

What is being done to make them a reality? _____
_____

How do you plan on documenting the journey? _____
_____

How would you rank this? ⭐⭐⭐⭐⭐ Why? _____
_____

#66 - Find your inner entrepreneurs

Start a small business together. Make and sell crafts or baked goods, mow lawns, or shovel sidewalks. Challenge your kids to get creative with products, marketing, and business strategies.

What kind of business did your family decide to start? _____
_____

What was done to market the product or service? _____
_____

What did the kids learn in the process? _____
_____

How would you rank this? ☆☆☆☆☆ Why? _____
_____

#67 - Cross the finish line together

Find a family-friendly race in your area that you can all do together. Develop a training schedule and hold each other accountable for following it. Cheer each other along on race day.

12 4 7

What race did you choose? _____
_____

What did the family do to train for it? _____
_____

How did everyone do on race day? _____
_____

How would you rank this? ☆☆☆☆☆ Why? _____
_____

Completed:

_____

#68 - Book a staycation

Reserve a hotel room close to home for a night or two. Pretend you're on a last-minute vacation out of town. Swim in the pool, go to the movies, eat out, and recharge your batteries without having to go too far from home.

Did everyone enjoy the mini vacation? _____

_____

What activities did you do? _____

_____

Where else could you go for a staycation? _____

_____

How would you rank this? ★ ★ ★ ★ ★ Why? _____

_____

#69 - Participate in a blind taste test

Pick a food with many varieties (i.e. ice cream, cheese, cereal, apples) and set out samples. Make forms to rank the food on various categories and tally the results to determine the favorite.

What type of food did you choose? _____

_____

What categories did you use to rank them? _____

_____

Which type/brand was the favorite? _____

_____

How would you rank this? ☆ ☆ ☆ ☆ ☆ Why? _____

_____

#70 - Learn something from each other

Put everyone's name in a hat and have each person draw a name. Then ask the person whose name you chose to teach you how to do something that they are really good at doing.

What did each person try to learn? _____

_____

How well did everyone pick up their new skill? _____

_____

Were there any surprise skills or abilities? _____

_____

How would you rank this? ★ ★ ★ ★ ★ Why? _____

_____

#71 - Discover a blast from the past

Take a trip to an antique store near you. Let your kids explore and find something that interests them. Seeing old toys, tools, and clothes is like a built in history lesson.

What things were most interesting? _____
_____

What kinds of questions did your kids ask? _____
_____

Did you do any research to learn more about you found? _____
_____

How would you rank this? ☆☆☆☆☆ Why? _____

Completed:
_____

#72 - Tune in to a new sound

Take turns picking out a new artist that you've never listened to before. Give the rest of the family a little background on the artist and make a playlist of the music for the family to listen to.

What new music did you listen to? _____
_____

What did you learn about the artists? _____
_____

Did you discover any new favorites? _____
_____

How would you rank this? ☆ ☆ ☆ ☆ ☆ Why? _____
_____

#73 - Document the everyday stuff

Have everyone take photos of the little, day-to-day stuff (i.e. your toothbrush color or the style of your gym shoes). Then print them out and create a collage to look back on in the years to come.

What things did you take pictures of? _____
_____

How did you assemble your photos? _____
_____

What do you think your favorite photo will be in ten years? _____
_____

How would you rank this? ☆☆☆☆☆ Why? _____
_____

Completed:
_____

Hi Mom

#74 - Write on the walls

Paint a section of wall, an old door, or a sheet of plywood with chalkboard paint. Put a frame around it and buy a bucket of colorful chalk. Leave each other messages, record your heights, draw pictures, play games, etc.

Where did you decide to make your chalkboard? _____
_____

How has your family used it? _____
_____

What is your favorite message or drawing so far? _____
_____

How would you rank this? ☆ ☆ ☆ ☆ ☆ Why? _____
_____

#75 - Figure out how something works

The next time something mechanical breaks, instead of throwing it out, take it apart. Inspect all the parts and pieces. Do a little research and see if you can figure out what makes it work.

What did you take apart? _____

_____

What did everyone learn about it? _____

_____

Was anyone able to get it working again? _____

_____

How would you rank this? ☆☆☆☆☆ Why? _____

_____

Completed:

_____

#76 - Scavenge your local library

Make a list of things you'd find in a library (i.e. an author with your same initials, a picture of a pyramid, or a quote about sea turtles). Vary the difficulty based on age and set a time limit.

What kinds of things did you search for? _____
_____

How many things did you cross off the list? _____
_____

What was the hardest to find? _____
_____

How would you rank this? ★ ★ ★ ★ ★ Why? _____
_____

Completed:
_____

#77 - Host your own gallery opening

Buy canvases and clay at a craft store. Have everyone draw, paint, or sculpt their own piece of art. Find an area of your house to display them. Invite friends over to unveil your masterpieces.

What medium did everyone choose? _____
_____

What was the inspiration for your creations? _____
_____

How was the unveiling party? _____
_____

How would you rank this? ☆ ☆ ☆ ☆ ☆ Why? _____
_____

#78 - Create a drive-in

Put up a screen or large sheet on your garage door or on the side of your building. Borrow a projector and pick a good family movie. When it gets dark, pile in the car with your favorite movie theater snacks and watch the show.

What movie did you watch? _____
_____

What did your family think of the experience? _____
_____

Would you consider hosting a drive-in for the neighbors? _____
_____

How would you rank this? ☆ ☆ ☆ ☆ ☆ Why? _____
_____

#79 - Reminisce about the good old days

Pull out your family's photo albums, home movies, and photos from your own childhood. Compare photos, laugh at how fashions have changed, and talk about your favorite memories together.

What did your family think of your photos? _____
_____

Did it bring back any good times that you'd forgotten? _____
_____

What are some of your favorite memories together? _____
_____

How would you rank this? ☆☆☆☆☆ Why? _____
_____

#80 - Get ready for back-to-school

Schedule one-on-one dates with your kids to pick up their school supplies and grocery trips for their lunches. The weekend before school starts throw a back-to-school BBQ with friends.

Did this help get the kids excited for school? _____

_____

How did they like the one-on-one time? _____

_____

What did you put together for the BBQ? _____

_____

How would you rank this? ☆ ☆ ☆ ☆ ☆ Why? _____

_____

#81 - Reconnect with nature, close to home

Surprise your family with a spontaneous camping weekend in the backyard. Pitch a tent, build a fort, or sleep under the stars. It's a great way to 'get away' and still have the comforts of home nearby.

How long did you camp? _____

_____

How did your family like staying outside? _____

_____

Did they learn any survival skills? Which ones? _____

_____

How would you rank this? ☆☆☆☆☆ Why? _____

_____

#82 - Play flashlight hide-and-seek

On the next warm night head outside. While one person counts, everyone else runs and hides. The first person found and 'tagged' with the flashlight has to take their turn as the seeker.

Was this more fun than regular hide-and-seek? _____
_____

How did your family like playing in the dark? _____
_____

Was it hard to find anyone? _____
_____

How would you rank this? ★ ★ ★ ★ ★ Why? _____
_____

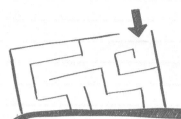

#83 - Remember the way through

Set up some large toys, chairs, etc in a yard or park. Have everyone take a look at the 'maze'. Then blindfold each person and see who can get the farthest, the fastest, without bumping into anything.

What did you use to create the maze? _____
_____

Did anyone make it all the way through? _____
_____

What was the fastest time? _____
_____

How would you rank this? ☆ ☆ ☆ ☆ ☆ Why? _____
_____

#84 - Keep in touch

Using a webcam and a free video chat program, such as Skype, set up some face-to-face time with relatives that your family does not get to see often. Try to make it a regular activity and make sure everyone participates.

Who have you been able to catch up with? _____

_____

What do your relatives think of the face-to-face time? _____

_____

How else could you keep in contact with them? _____

_____

How would you rank this? ☆ ☆ ☆ ☆ ☆ Why? _____

_____

#85 - Pick-your-own

Take the family out to a pick-your-own farm. Try a day in the apple orchards in the fall or a blueberry patch in the summer. Head home with your produce and find recipes to make together with what you've picked.

What type of farm did you go to? _____
_____

What did your family pick? _____
_____

What did you make from your fresh produce? _____
_____

How would you rank this? ☆☆☆☆☆ Why? _____
_____

#86 - Whip up some homemade ice cream

Make your favorite flavors with only a few ingredients. You don't need a fancy machine; just look online for directions. Turn it into a science lesson and explain how matter changes states as you go.

What flavor(s) did you make? _____
_____

Was it easy enough to do regularly? _____
_____

What did your family learn in the process? _____
_____

How would you rank this? ☆ ☆ ☆ ☆ ☆ Why? _____
_____

#87 - Make a splash

Find an indoor water park in your area and enjoy some slip-sliding fun with your family, no matter the time of year. There's something for all ages, from big slides to wade pools, and it's a great way to break up the winter blahs.

Which water park did you go to? _____
_____

What was everyone's favorite part? _____
_____

Did the trip help anyone feel more comfortable in the water?
_____

How would you rank this? ☆ ☆ ☆ ☆ ☆ Why? _____
_____

#88 - Be card sharks

Get out a deck of cards and teach your kids how to play some classic card games (i.e. hearts, euchre, rummy, canasta). For little kids start with go fish or Uno. If your kids are older, raise the stakes and introduce them to poker.

Which card games did you play? _____

_____

What was everyone's favorite game? _____

_____

Was anyone interested in learning more card games? _____

_____

How would you rank this? ★ ★ ★ ★ ★ Why? _____

_____

Completed:

_____

#89 - Use your senses

Create a sensory table using large bowls or bins filled with objects that have different textures (i.e. peeled grapes, cold spaghetti, cotton balls). Blindfold each person. Have them describe what they feel and guess what the objects are.

What objects did you put in the bins? _____

_____

Which was the hardest to guess? _____

_____

Which was the easiest to guess? _____

_____

How would you rank this? ☆ ☆ ☆ ☆ ☆ Why? _____

_____

#90 - Take storytime on the road

Gather up random objects in your house and divide them among a few paper bags. Store them in your car. The next time the kids get bored have them come up with a story based on the items in their bag.

What items did you put in each bag? _____

_____

How creative were the kids with their stories? _____

_____

What other objects could you put in the bags? _____

_____

How would you rank this? ☆ ☆ ☆ ☆ ☆ Why? _____

_____

#91 - Shop smarter

Search online for free classes at retailers in your area and learn anything from craft projects to making your own videos. Stores like Lowe's, Michaels, and Apple have great workshops for everyone in the family.

Where did you find classes? _____
_____

Which classes did your family decide to try? _____
_____

What did everyone learn? _____
_____

How would you rank this? ☆☆☆☆☆ Why? _____
_____

#92 - Conduct yearly interviews

Come up with a list of questions to ask each person every year on their birthday (i.e. favorite color, shoe size, best friend). Put all of the answers and a picture in a keepsake journal.

What kinds of questions did you ask? _____
_____

How did they change for each family member? _____
_____

How did your family feel about answering them? _____
_____

How would you rank this? ☆ ☆ ☆ ☆ ☆ Why? _____
_____

#93 - Watch a classic

Find some old cartoons or a movie that you used to love watching when you were a kid. Gather up the family and have a throwback TV night. See how your old shows stack up to your family's current favorites.

What are your favorite old-school shows/movies? _____
_____

What did your family think about them? _____
_____

Did you establish any 'new' family favorites? _____
_____

How would you rank this? ☆☆☆☆☆ Why? _____
_____

#94 - Try your hand at watercolors

On the next rainy day get out the rain gear and side walk chalk and head out to the drive way. In the rain, the chalk works like paint. Have a great time blending and mixing colors.

How did everyone like playing in the rain? _____

_____

What did they draw? _____

_____

How did it compare to drawing with dry chalk? _____

_____

How would you rank this? ★ ★ ★ ★ ★ Why? _____

_____

Completed: _____

#95 - Keep some things in the family

Come up with a cool family handshake, silly inside joke, or a secret code. Make it a ritual that you share only with your family members. It makes it special to have something exclusive to you.

What did you come up with? _____
_____

When do you use it? _____
_____

What does the family think about it? _____
_____

How would you rank this? ☆ ☆ ☆ ☆ ☆ Why? _____
_____

HA HAHA
HA

#96 - Work on your comedic timing

Designate a classic joke day once a week. Take turns coming up with a joke (i.e. knock knock, riddles, puns) and share it with the family before everyone leaves in the morning or during family dinners.

What types of jokes did everyone come up with? _____
_____

What's the favorite joke so far? _____
_____

Does it help set a good tone for the day? How? _____
_____

How would you rank this? ☆ ☆ ☆ ☆ ☆ Why? _____
_____

#97 - Make a trade

Gather up some things that your family is tired of, but not quite ready to give away (i.e. toys, books, clothes, movies). Invite some friends and family over to exchange their boring, 'old' items for fun, 'new' items.

What things were your family ready to swap? _____
_____

What 'new' things did they get in return? _____
_____

Did they forget about their 'old' stuff or want it back? _____
_____

How would you rank this? ☆☆☆☆☆ Why? _____
_____

Completed:

_____

#98 - Walk in the park

Visit some of the nation's most beautiful and awe-inspiring sites. Go online to www.nps.gov and search for national parks near you as well as free entrance days. Many are free to visit every day of the year!

Which park(s) did you decide to visit? _____

_____

What did your family think about the park? _____

_____

Was it nearby or did you have to travel? _____

_____

How would you rank this? ☆ ☆ ☆ ☆ ☆ Why? _____

_____

#99 - Break out the spray cans

Have a whipped cream fight! Head outside with a can for each person and let the kids loose. Don't forget to take a photo of your sticky, sweet family and make sure you have a hose nearby.

How did your family react to this? _____
_____

How much was eaten rather than sprayed on others? _____
_____

Who got covered the most? _____
_____

How would you rank this? ☆☆☆☆☆ Why? _____
_____

#100 - See yourself the way others do

Trace the silhouette of each person on a roll of paper, and cut them out. Have everyone write notes and paste pictures representing what they love and admire about them on each other's silhouette.

What kinds of things were written? _____
_____

Were there any surprises? _____
_____

How did it make them feel to see their finished silhouette?
_____

How would you rank this? ★ ★ ★ ★ ★ Why? _____
_____